Pinocchio

Adapted by
Eve Leigh

T0348009

methuen | drama

LONDON · NEW YORK · OXFORD · NEW DELHI · SYDNEY

METHUEN DRAMA
Bloomsbury Publishing Plc
50 Bedford Square, London, WC1B 3DP, UK
1385 Broadway, New York, NY 10018, USA
29 Earlsfort Terrace, Dublin 2, Ireland

BLOOMSBURY, METHUEN DRAMA and the Methuen Drama logo
are trademarks of Bloomsbury Publishing Plc

First published in Great Britain 2022

A catalogue record for this book is available from the British Library.

A catalog record for this book is available from the Library of Congress.

ISBN: PB: 978-1-3503-8430-9
ePDF: 978-1-3503-8431-6
eBook: 978-1-3503-8432-3

Series Plays for Young People

Typeset by Newgen KnowledgeWorks Pvt. Ltd., Chennai, India

To find out more about our authors and books visit
www.bloomsbury.com and sign up for our newsletters.

THE UK'S THEATRE FOR YOUNG AUDIENCES

PINOCCHIO

Adapted by Eve Leigh

This production of *Pinocchio* was produced by the Unicorn Theatre and opened in November 2022.

With special thanks to Charles Holloway, the Unicorn Theatre's Christmas Production Partner

Cast and Company

Susan Harrison	**Marmalade**
Tom Kanji	**Geppetto/Fratello**
Sam Pay	**Mommo**
Peyvand Sadeghian	**Pinocchio**
Eleanor Wyld	**Polpetta/Duchess/Blue Fairy**

Adapted by Eve Leigh
Directed by Justin Audibert
Designed by Jean Chan
Movement and Puppetry Direction by Laura Cubitt
Lighting Design by Ric Mountjoy
Composed by Barnaby Race
Sound Design by Ed Clarke
Puppet Design and Make by Chris Pirie
Associate Designed by Pip Terry
Costume Supervised by Lydia Hardiman
Arrangements by Samuel Wilson
Puppet Fabrication by Izzy Bristow
Blinks and Twinkles by Nick Willsher

Production Manager	**Jennifer Taillefer**
Stage Manager	**Rosalind Doré**
Deputy Stage Manager	**Sarah Lyndon**
Assistant Stage Manager	**Chloe Jones**
Stage Management Placement	**Ellie Holloway**

Susan Harrison | Performer

Susan trained at The Royal Conservatoire of Scotland. TV credits include: *Class Dismissed* (CBBC); *Definitely Not Newsround* (CBBC). Theatre includes: *Mischief Movie Night* (Riverside Studios); *Peter Pan Goes Wrong* (Mischief Theatre / West End); *The Elephantom* (National Theatre); *Showstopper! The Improvised Musical* (West End and on tour); *Robin Hood and Marian* (New Vic Theatre); *Heels of Glory* (Chelsea Theatre); *Bagpuss* (Soho Theatre); *The Gathering* (Theatre Abandon); *Hansel & Gretel* (National Theatre of Scotland / Catherine Wheels); *Men Should Weep* (Oxford Stage Company); *Cinderella, Aladdin* (Corn Exchange Newbury); *The Fence* (Wrestling School); *Bad Girls* (Polka Theatre/Watershed Productions); *The BFG* (Polka Theatre); *Charlie and Lola* (Polka Theatre/BBC Worldwide). Radio includes: *Gemma Arrowsmith: Emergency Broadcast* (BBC Radio 4); *The Simon Day Show* (BBC Radio 4). Susan is a member of *Showstopper! The Improvised Musical* & a co-creator of *These Folk*, a two-person improvised folk musical.

Tom Kanji | Performer

Tom trained at RADA. Theatre includes: *Private Peaceful* (Nottingham Playhouse); *Home I'm Darling* (Keswick); *Shoe Lady* (Royal Court); *Yes Prime Minister* (Theatre Clwyd); *Midsummer Night's Dream, Macbeth* (Shakespeare's Rose); *Richard III* (Headlong); *Love's Labour's Lost, Winter's Tale, Pericles, Romeo and Juliet, Julius Caesar, Dr Scroggy's War, Eternal Love* (Shakespeare's Globe); *Country Wife* (Chichester); *Taming of the Shrew* (US Tour); *Box of Delights* (Wilton's); *Fiddler on the Roof, Romeo and Juliet, Story Giant, The Sum* (Liverpool Everyman); *Romeo and Juliet, Anthony and Cleopatra, Much Ado About Nothing* (Barbican); *Much Ado About Nothing, Twelfth Night* (Ludlow); *Hamlet* (Northern Broadsides); *Tempest* (Tara Arts); *Les Liaisons Dangereuses* (New Vic Stoke); *Indian Ink* (Salisbury Playhouse). Television includes: *Supercell* (Netflix); *Tyrant* (Fox); *Silent Witness, Hustle* (BBC); *Midnight Man* (ITV); *Saddam's Tribe* (Channel 4).

Sam Pay | Performer

Sam is an actor-musician based in South London. Trained at ALRA in Wandsworth, he spent several years as part of the cut to the chase company at The Queen's Theatre Hornchurch, as well as appearing at the Royal Shakespeare Company in 2018 and 2019. He co-hosts the award-winning music analysis podcast Song by Song every week. Theatre credits include: *Merchant of Venice, Tamburlaine, Timon of Athens, Tartuffe* (Royal Shakespeare Company); *The Wind In The Willows* (Colchester Mercury); *Much Ado About Nothing, The Great Gatsby, Godspell* (Queen's Theatre Hornchurch); *Trelawney Of The Wells, Privates on Parade* (Pitlochry Festival Theatre); *The BFG* (UK Tour).

Peyvand Sadeghian | Performer

Peyvand is an actor, puppeteer and theatremaker who has performed for family audiences nationwide including at York Theatre Royal, Derby Theatre, Little Angel Theatre and Lyric Hammersmith. Training includes: National Youth Theatre GB, BA (hons) Drama & Theatre Arts, Goldsmiths, University of London. Theatre credits include: *Dual* دوگاﻧﻪ (Vault Festival); *Rich Kids: A History of Shopping Malls in Tehran* (UK and International tour). Screen credits include: *Queen Charlotte: A Bridgerton Story* (Netflix); *Moon Knight* (Marvel); *Pirates* (Netflix); *The Power* (Amazon).

Eleanor Wyld | Performer

Eleanor Wyld trained at Guildhall. Her stage credits include: *Merchant of Venice* (Sam Wanamaker Playhouse); *Leopoldstadt* (West End); *Don Juan in Soho* (West End); *The Ballad of Corona V* (Big House Theatre); *About Leo* (Jermyn St); *Hamlet* (Royal Shakespeare Company UK and US tour / Hackney Empire); *Don Quixote* (RSC / West End); *Doctor Faustus, The Alchemist* (Royal Shakespeare Company / Barbican); *Visitors* (Arcola / Bush Theatre); *Dances of Death* (Gate Theatre). Television credits include: *Trigonometry* (BBC); *Love Sick* (Netflix); *Misfits* (Channel 4); *Thirteen* (BBC). Film credits include: *The Critic; Bonobo; Frequencies*.

Eve Leigh | Writer

Eve is a writer for performance. Plays include *Flächenbrand* (Theater Bonn); *Midnight Movie* (Royal Court); *While You Are Here* (The Place/Dance East); *The Trick* (Bush Theatre, national tour); *Spooky Action at a Distance* (Royal Court / RWCMD); *The Curtain* (Young Vic Taking Part); *Stone Face, Silent Planet* (Finborough Theatre). Game, installation and digital credits include: *Words Fail: A Fortune Telling Game* (Coney); *Ghost Pine* (Audible); *The Delegation* (Coney / Точка доступа); *Invisible Summer* (Royal Court); *Movimento / Variations* (36 маймуни / Bulgarian National Theatre Festival); *Your Future* (HAU / Sophiensaele / Ballhaus Ost / Camden People's Theatre); *A Short and Boring Story* (Camden People's Theatre). Residencies include Royal Court 2019 and 2017, Experimental Stage of the National Theatre of Greece 2017, AIDF Teatr Polski Bydgoszcz 2016. Awards include Berlin Theatertreffen Stueckemarkt selection 2021, Sarah Award for Audio Fiction 2020, Jerwood / Royal Court New Playwright Award 2019 (with Jasmine Lee-Jones), Women's Prize for Playwriting Finalist 2020, Bruntwood Prize shortlist 2019. She is an associate artist at Coney.

Justin Audibert | Director

Justin Audibert is Artistic Director of the Unicorn Theatre. Most recently, he has created and directed *Marvin's Binoculars* for the Unicorn Theatre, as well as the *Guardians of the Galaxy* Secret Cinema experience. Over the last 18 months, Justin has worked in partnership with the National Theatre to deliver *Story Seekers*: a free six-week creative literacy project for state school years 4–6, which focuses on supporting children to develop their communication and language skills post-pandemic. Previous directing credits include: *Anansi the Spider; The Canterville Ghost; Aesop's Fables* (Unicorn Theatre); *The Taming of the Shrew, The Snow in Midsummer, The Jew of Malta* (Royal Shakespeare Company); *Macbeth, The Winter's Tale* (National Theatre).

Jean Chan | Designer

Graduating in 2008 from the Royal Welsh College of Music and Drama. Jean went on to work as a resident designer, part of the Royal Shakespeare Company's Trainee Design Programme 2008–09. In 2009 she won the Linbury Prize for Stage Design, with an adaptation of Elizabeth Laird's *Garbage King* produced at the Unicorn Theatre in 2010. Design credits include: *The Meaning of Zong* (Bristol Old Vic); *Twelfth Night, A Midsummer Night's Dream* (Shakespeare's Globe); *Reason You Should(n't) Love Me* (Kiln Theatre); *Wild Goose, Plastic* (Theatre Royal Bath); *Dick Whittington, Jack and the Beanstalk* (Lyric Hammersmith); *The Witches, James and the Giant Peach, The BFG* (Dundee Rep); *Jumpy, Hedda Gabler* (The Royal Lyceum, Edinburgh); *Petula, Mother Courage* (National Theatre Wales). Costume Design credits include: *Legally Blonde* (Regent's Park Open Air Theatre); *Knights' Tale* (Toho Theatre, Japan); *The Grinning Man* (Trafalgar Studio / Bristol Old Vic); *Lionboy* (Complicite).

Laura Cubitt | Movement and Puppetry Director

Laura is a Puppetry Director, Movement Director and Performer. Directing credits include: *Dragons and Mythical Beasts* (Regent's Park Open Air Theatre & tour, Olivier Award nominated). Puppetry credits include: *A Monster Calls* (Chichester Festival Theatre); *The Boy in the Dress* (RSC); *The Little Prince* (Fuel); *Don Quixote* (RSC); *A Monster Calls* (The Old Vic / Bristol Old Vic); *Small Island, Common* (National Theatre); *Dinosaur World Live* (Nicoll); *Rudolph* (Birmingham Mac); *The Curious Incident of the Dog in the Night-Time* (National Theatre / West End – Puppetry Consultancy); *Macbeth* (Red Rose Chain); *Running Wild* (Chichester Festival Theatre – Associate Puppetry Director); *Goodnight Mr Tom* (West End – Associate Puppetry Director). Movement credits include: *Run Sister Run* (Paines Plough); *Anna* (National Theatre – Associate Movement Director); *Oppenheimer* (Royal Shakespeare Company / West End – Movement Re-Staging); *War Horse* (NT Berlin – Associate Movement Director); *2012 Olympics Opening* (Associate Movement Director).

Ric Mountjoy | Lighting Designer

Ric designs lighting for theatre and opera, and his work has been seen all over the world: from Singapore to Seattle, Dubai to Dhaka, and most significantly in London and New York City. Recent lighting designs include: *The Play that Goes Wrong* on Broadway (Lyceum Theatre) and in the West End (Duchess Theatre – 2015 Olivier Award for Best New Comedy); *Father* by Akram Khan (Dhaka, Bangladesh); *Oi Frog + Friends* (West End & UK Tour); *Uncle Vanya* (Theatr Clwyd & Sheffield Theatres); *Darbar Festival* (Akram Khan Company & Sadler's Wells); *Mr Popper's Penguins* (New York City, Minneapolis & West End); *Emancipation of Expressionism* (Boy Blue Entertainment, Barbican Theatre, & BBC TV); *Zog* (UK Tour); *The White Whale* – an outdoor adaptation of Moby Dick (Slung Low, Leeds); and *What the Ladybird Heard* (International Touring). Ric worked for many years at English National Opera, and before that for Birmingham Royal Ballet.

Barnaby Race | Composer

Selected composer and musical supervisor credits include: *The Lion, The Witch and The Wardrobe* (The Gillian Lynne Theatre, Composer/Musical Supervisor); *Peaky Blinders: The Rise* (Immersive Everywhere, Composer Musical Supervisor); *Amélie* (Criterion Theatre, Musical Supervisor, nominated for the Olivier Award for 'Original Score or New Orchestration' and the Grammy Award as co-producer for Best Musical Theater Album); *Doctor Who: Time Fracture* (Songwriter/Lyricist, Immersive Everywhere); *Cinderella: A New Musical* (Nuffield, Southampton. Composer and Additional Lyrics); *A Christmas Carol* (Theatre Clwyd, Composer); *The Secret Garden* (Theatre by the Lake/York Theatre Royal, Composer); *Romeo + Juliet* and *One Flew Over The Cuckoo's Nest* (Secret Cinema, Composer/Musical Supervisor); *The Last Days of Anne Boleyn* (Historic Royal Palaces/Tower of London, Composer); *Babe, The Sheep-Pig* (Polka Theatre/UK Tour, Composer); *Pine* (Hampstead Theatre, Composer); *Minotaur* (Polka Theatre/Theatre Clwyd, Composer); *How to be Immortal* (Soho Theatre/UK Tour, Composer); *Cesario* (National Theatre, Assistant Musical Director).

Ed Clarke | Sound Designer
Ed Clarke's work in theatre includes: *Baddies* (Unicorn Theatre); *Doncastrian Chalk Circle* (National Theatre Public Acts); *Frankenstein* and *The Mysteries* (National Theatre); *Wolf Witch Giant Fairy* (Royal Opera House); *Nine Lives* (Bridge Theatre); *All We Ever Wanted Was Everything, Us Against Whatever, Canary and the Crow* (Middle Child Theatre); *A Christmas Carol* and *Oliver Twist* (Hull Truck); *An Adventure, Leave Taking, The Royale, Perseverance Drive* and *The Invisible* (Bush Theatre); *The Infidel* (Theatre Royal, Stratford East); *Orpheus* (Battersea Arts Centre, Salzburg Festival); *Beauty and the Beast* (Young Vic); *The Railway Children* (Waterloo International Station and Roundhouse Theatre, Toronto); *Backbeat* (Duke Of York's Theatre) and *Showboat* (New London Theatre).

Chris Pirie | Puppetry Designer & Maker
Chris is a puppetry director, designer and performer, and is the Artistic Director of leading European theatre company Green Ginger. Alongside co-creating the company's design-led ensemble productions, he has directed productions for Tobacco Factory Theatres, Scamp Productions and Travelling Light. Chris has also directed and designed puppetry solutions for Unicorn Theatre, Arcadia Spectacular, Lyric Opera Chicago, Bristol Old Vic, Kneehigh Theatre, Theatr Iolo, Royal & Derngate, Theatr Sherman, Opera di Roma, Teatro di Communale Bologna, Welsh National Opera, Canadian Opera Company, San Francisco Opera, Houston Grand Opera and the Norwegian National Opera. Film and TV credits include puppetry for Netflix, Aardman Animations, BBC and Channel 5. Chris is a Fellow of the Higher Education Academy and lectures at Bath Spa University, Curious School of Puppetry and other leading UK academic institutions. He co-founded Bristol Festival of Puppetry, and created *Toast in the Machine*; a mentorship program for emerging UK and US puppeteers.

Pip Terry | Associate Designer

Pip Terry works as a set and costume designer and design Assistant. She graduated from Wimbledon College of Arts in 2020 and was awarded the Linbury Prize for Stage Design in 2021. Pip is currently employed as the Kiln Theatre's Resident assistant designer. Theatre credits include: As Assistant: *Black Love* (Kiln Theatre), *Girl on an Altar* (Kiln Theatre), *The Darkest Part of the Night* (Kiln Theatre), *Handbagged* (Kiln Theatre), *Kerry Jackson* (National Theatre). Associate credits include: *Splintered* (Soho Theatre), *Tempest* (RSC). As Designer: *Sticks and Stones* (Tristan Bates Theatre), *The House at the Centre of the World* (Rose Theatre), *The Normal World* (The Place), *Ad Nauseam* (Lyric Hammersmith's Evolution Festival). Pip has also worked on *Disney's Frozen* (Theatre Royal Drury Lane), *Moulin Rouge!* (Piccadilly Theatre) and *Death of England* (National Theatre) as a scenic painter and prop maker's assistant.

THE UK'S THEATRE FOR YOUNG AUDIENCES

Unicorn Theatre

At the Unicorn we create new, inventive and enthralling theatre experiences for children aged up to 13, offering an inspiring year-round programme of shows. Every year, we welcome around 65,000 families and schools through our doors, and many thousands more through Unicorn Online. We believe that young people of all ages, perspectives and abilities have the right to experience exciting, entertaining and inspiring work and we actively seek out children who wouldn't otherwise attend, offering free tickets where needed. We develop work with children from our partner schools and community groups to ensure that our work remains relevant and informed by the young people we serve. Our values of courage, curiosity and respect run through everything we do.

Royal Patron

The former Duchess of Cornwall

Honorary Patrons

Joanna David
David Isaacs
Giles Havergal CBE

Board of Directors

Dr Vanessa Ogden (Chair)
Simon Davidson
Dominic Griffiths
Axa Hynes
Henny Finch
Prema Mehta
Colin Simon
Piers Torday

Unicorn Theatre Team

Artistic Director	Justin Audibert
Co-Executive Director	Bailey Lock
Co-Executive Director	Helen Tovey
Associate Director (**freelance**)	Rachel Bagshaw
Artistic Associate (**freelance**)	Jean Chan
Senior Producer	Katie Shahatit
Producer	Sair Smith
Producing and Production Assistant	Joseph Winer
Engagement Director	Georgia Dale
Engagement Producer	Shanti Sarkar
Engagement Assistant	Jahmila Heath
General Manager	Amy Smith
Finance Director	Ida Karimi
Finance Manager	Marianna Zicari
Technical and Production Director	Ria Tubman
Technical Manager	Rob Johnson
Senior Technician	Kiri Baildon-Smith
Venue Technicians	Bernadette Ward, Lucas Leao
Company Stage Manager	Sophie Sierra
Facilities Manager (**Interim**)	Rhys Cannon
Stage Door Administrator	Allen McGlynn
Stage Door Keepers	Suzie Digby, Chris Mayo, Julie Patten, Nathan Queeley-Dennis, Alice Wilson, Rob Wilson, TJ Wilson
Director of Development	Lucy Buxton
Development Manager (**Trusts and Foundations**)	Anna Lyttle
Development Officer	Lily Easton
Director of Marketing and Communications	Jen Pearce
Marketing Manager	Nathan Picart
Schools Relationship Officer	Frey Kwa Hawking
Marketing Assistant	Gehna Badhwar
Press and PR (**freelance**)	Clióna Roberts, CRPR

Front of House Manager	Ella Becker
Box Office Manager	Rhys Evans
Deputy Sales and Performance Manager	James Darby
Performance Managers	Alex Dowding, Bobby Wilkinson, Alice Wilson
Box Office Assistants	Annie Kershaw, Chris Mayo, Joel Oladapo, Nathan Queeley-Dennis, Shannon Fox, Tilly-Jane Wilson.
Senior Front of House Assistant	Matthew Newell
Front of House Assistant	Alicia Walker, Bambi Phillips, Ben Wilson, Beverley Cramb, Carole Mitchell, Dan Gee, Eleanor Mack, Ezra Joy, Grace Malloch, Henrietta Thomas, Howes Reynolds, DJ Hassan, Isobel Tyrell, Jackie Downer, Jamie Maier, Juliette Moore, Kathryn Bates, Laura Wheeler, Lizzie Corscaden, Malika Quintyne, Mariana Macías Márquez, Matthew Newell, Megan Brodie, Merlin Hayward, Naomi Denny, Neave Matthews, Nor Leinster, Reanna Bongo, Renecia Allen, Robert Pearce, Robert Wilson, Ruby Carbonell, Soline Smith, Sophie Underwood, Suzie Digby, Tianna Haffenden.

Supported using public funding by
**ARTS COUNCIL
ENGLAND**

Pinocchio

Characters

Pinocchio, *a wooden doll*
Geppetto, *an old man with a grey beard*
Marmalade, *a cat*
The **Blue Fairy**, *who has more in common with a sarcastic old Jewish man than you might expect*
Polpetta, *a permanently sticky little girl stuffed into an immaculate ruffly dress*
Fratello, *a fine-looking gent with a glittery gold beard*
Mommo, *a dreadful bully*
The **Conscience**, *a mosquito, portrayed by a sound cue*
The **Duchess**
The **Dogfish**, *a monstrous puppet*
Geppetto and Fratello are played by the same person
Polpetta, the Blue Fairy and the Duchess are all played by the same person

Setting

A small, gingerbready village near the forest, in the Italian Alps, as autumn becomes winter.

Once upon a time.

Act One

Scene One

Marmalade, *an uncommonly sleek and handsome ginger cat, is alone, centre stage.*

Marmalade   Once upon a time –

There was ME, Marmalade the Cat!

The musician stops playing and coughs loudly, looking sternly at **Marmalade**.

Marmalade   Once upon a time – (*hurrying to the end of the sentence so as not to be interrupted*) there was ME, Marmalade the Cat living in the home of a master toymaker, Geppetto!

A beat. No objection from offstage.

Geppetto could make anything you like out of wood, so well that it looked real – he carved a tree out of wood for me to climb on, right in the middle of his house, and you may say – well, carving a TREE out of WOOD that looks real, that's not very hard surely?

But no. He carved it so in the middle of his house it looked like there was a living tree, every dip and ebb of the bark, every little ant crawling on the surface, looked so real that sometimes I forget and jump on the ants, even though I've done it a million times, there's something about the way the tree trunk looks in the firelight that I am just sure – this time – the ants are real.

He loved me very much.

But there was something sad about his love, something very sad – and I never knew what it was.

But I could see it, you know? I could see it in the way he scritched my chin in the mornings, and the way he shooed me out of his workshop when it was gonna be very dusty with wood shavings.

But I never knew what the sadness was.

Until –

Pinocchio *appears. He is not animate yet – a wooden doll with articulated joints, slumped against a wall. He has a small, round halo of hair, made of twigs, and a perfectly round little nose, like a miniature button mushroom.*

Marmalade   Geppetto made a very large toy, that looked just like a child.

Geppetto *appears, painting it, putting on finishing touches.* **Marmalade** *is curious about it and has a sniff.*

Marmalade   But it wasn't a child, it was a toy like the other toys.

Geppetto *stares at it intently. He gets back to other work, sanding a bench.*

Marmalade *flops down in front of him and shows his belly.*

Geppetto *scritches* **Marmalade**'s *little belly, sadly.*

Geppetto   Will I ever have a child?

A child to love. To carry on the family name.

This is stupid, a grown man, making himself a doll!

I can't look at it!

Geppetto *throws a tarp over* **Pinocchio**.

Marmalade *and* **Gepetto** *look at the tarp.*

Geppetto   Too sad.

Geppetto *takes the tarp off.*

Pinocchio *is slouched on his side, looking like the inanimate doll he is.*

But also quite a lot like a child.

Geppetto   Or is *that* too sad?

Geppetto *straightens him up.*

Somehow, when **Pinocchio** *is sitting up, he looks both more and less like a human being.*

Geppetto   Oh I don't know, I don't know.

Geppetto *gingerly tucks the tarp around him, as if* **Pinocchio** *was sitting up in bed.*

Geppetto   Oh I can't look at him any more!

Geppetto *blows out the candles in his little cottage and gets into bed. A fat blue moon rises above the cottage. The forest is black, and the snowy Alps shine blue in the starlight.*

Marmalade   But late that night, as I was on the roof frightening the squirrels, I heard …

Geppetto   I wish.

I wish I could have a child.

I wish on the blue moon, with my whole heart.

Marmalade   And I knew that something big was going to happen.

Geppetto   I wish to be a parent.

Scene Two

The moon gets bigger and bigger. And bluer and bluer. Until finally a beautiful **Blue Fairy** *emerges from the moon and comes into the nighttime cottage.*

Blue Fairy   If you make a wish with your whole heart on a blue moon night, sometimes the Blue Fairy can hear you.

And tonight is a blue moon.

And I am the Blue Fairy!

Geppetto   What's happening?

Blue Fairy   I see this little wooden child, tucked up.

Geppetto   That's not a wooden child.

It's a – duck.

Blue Fairy   How is it a duck?

Geppetto   The er.

The nose, you see.

It's a duck in a little hat.

Blue Fairy   Ah OK.

Well if you don't actually want a real child – if this is a duck in a little hat – then I suppose I'll just go about my business –

Geppetto   NO NO NO it's, it's something I made because I thought if, if I could take care of something, oh I want a child so badly, please don't leave.

Blue Fairy   Why did you lie to me?

Geppetto   I don't know.

I've always wanted to be a parent, and –

I thought I'd made my peace, it's, you know, it won't happen.

But OH IT'S JUST SO EMBARRASSING, isn't it!

I'm a grown-up! I shouldn't be making – toys! That I wish were real!

Blue Fairy   It may be embarrassing but you shouldn't lie about it.

If you don't tell the truth, you can't be loved.

Geppetto   You can't / be loved –?

Blue Fairy   You only get one wish on the blue moon. Only one wish, in your whole life. So – tell me what your wish is, the REAL wish, the wish of your heart, the one wish of your entire life.

Geppetto   My real wish, the one wish of my entire life, is to have a child, and be a good parent to them.

Blue Fairy   I will grant your wish. (**Geppetto** *can't believe it*.) But!

We're gonna have to have you on a little probation period. You and the kid.

For now, he will be a wooden toy, that can walk and talk and – have a soul, be a bit of a person.

If, by Christmas, he's learned to be good, to tell the truth, then he will become a REAL boy. Like this one here (*indicates a boy in the audience*).

But if you can't teach him that – if you're not a good enough parent – his soul will disappear. He'll be nothing but firewood. And that will be the end of your one wish, and your chance to be a parent.

Geppetto   I'll do that! I'll take such good care of him. I will.

Blue Fairy   Very confident I see. No need for any extra help then?

Geppetto   I want every scrap of help you can possibly ever give me.

Blue Fairy   Good.

Here's one thing. When he lies, you'll definitely be able to tell.

Geppetto   How?

Blue Fairy (*looks at the audience*)   Don't worry about it.

And he'll have a little extra help too, wherever he goes.

A buzzing sound zooms in.

Blue Fairy   Hear that?

Geppetto   A mosquito?

But it's winter.

Blue Fairy   Yes, for now, this mosquito will be his conscience. It'll buzz if he's acting up. But he'll respond to it however he likes. Remember, it's about telling the truth and being good, not about being obedient.

What is the doll's name?

Geppetto   ... Pinocchio.

Blue Fairy   Pinocchio.

Well, your choice I suppose.

A light passes from the **Blue Fairy** *to* **Pinocchio**, *like a little blue flame.*

Marmalade   But just then a cloud covered the big blue moon, and the Blue Fairy vanished.

Geppetto *approaches the doll carefully, confused about whether to wake him up or not, scared of being taken for a fool –*

Pinocchio   Papa?

Geppetto   ... No ... !

Pinocchio   Papa? Is that you?

Pinocchio *removes the tarp from his legs and stands up. There's something cute about him, like a baby goat taking his first steps.*

Geppetto   My child, my boy.

My deepest wish has come true.

Scene Three

Marmalade   So Geppetto made some hot chocolate for the two of them, and put out a little goat's milk for me, and he told Pinocchio about the world.

Geppetto   This is Marmalade. Marmalade's a cat, and if you look out that window, you see those snowy things against the sky, those are mountains. We live by the sea, oh the sea, you're going to love the sea, unless you're scared of it, that would be ok if you're scared of it, but you'll probably love it I think. There's a castle where the mountains meet the sea, the Duchess lives there with her terrible daughter, you'll see it in the morning, you can't miss it, it's the only castle for miles. It's winter, or it's coming on winter now, which means the earth's getting colder, but it'll get warmer again in time. Time. Right. Time is –

Pinocchio   Papa –

Geppetto   (Oh, Papa, I've wanted to be called Papa for so long.) Yes what?

Pinocchio   What's the difference between me and a real boy?

Geppetto   I don't really know, Pinocchio.

Except that I made you out of wood, and most children are made – another way.

Pinocchio   Will I ever be a real boy?

Geppetto   You could be! You could be as soon as Christmas! But you need to be a good boy, not lie, and listen to your conscience.

Pinocchio   What's a conscience?

Geppetto   It's what tells you right from wrong. Your conscience is a mosquito, it buzzes around when you're doing something wrong.

Pinocchio   How will I tell right from wrong?

Geppetto   Well I just told you, your conscience will tell you.

Pinocchio   What if my conscience doesn't work?

Geppetto   Your conscience always works.

Pinocchio   Always always?

Geppetto   Well ... nearly always.

Pinocchio   So – it doesn't always work?!

Geppetto   Look, don't you want to know about the mountains, and night, and time?

Pinocchio   Er ... yes, but –

Geppetto   This is nighttime. People sleep in the nighttime. If people don't sleep in the nighttime they get cranky.

Pinocchio   What's cranky?

Geppetto   It's er –

It's how we sometimes get when someone small that we love is asking us loads of questions but we need to go to sleep.

Pinocchio   What's sleep?

Geppetto   Oh, sleep!

He folds out a lovely bedroll, invitingly.

Sleep is lovely, why don't you try some nice sleep, and we can talk some more in the morning. The nights are drawing in, it's not long til the busy season for toymakers, I need rest!

Pinocchio (*sleepily*)   Papa –

Geppetto's *heart lifts.*

Pinocchio   What if my conscience – what if it gets hurt or lost? Or –

Will I never be a real boy?

Geppetto   Go to sleep now, Pinocchio.

Real boys need their sleep.

Marmalade   And Geppetto and Pinocchio both went off to sleep like that, you know how humans are when they've had a bit of excitement.

Scene Four

Geppetto *and* **Pinocchio** *are in front of the cottage, by the sea.*

Geppetto   There it is.

Pinocchio   It's like a monster with a million eyes!

Geppetto   Once it gets warmer we'll go swimming in it. If – if we, if, you're a good enough boy, and I'm a good enough parent. And we, you know. We're all here in summer. (*Shudders at the thought of* **Pinocchio** *not being here.*) Oh, I don't even want to think about that!

Pinocchio   Can't we go swimming now?

Geppetto   No.

Or – we could I suppose, but I don't want to, it'd be so cold! I think it's a bit dangerous to go swimming when it's this cold actually, I think you can get stunned and get into difficulties.

Maybe not if you're made of wood, though, I don't know. We're so soft, me and Marmalade, flesh is so soft, you might be an absolute trooper in the sea, I suppose.

Pinocchio *has a mischievous idea* – **Pinocchio** *pushes* **Geppetto** *a little.*

Pinocchio   What if I fell in the sea? Or you pushed me in?

Geppetto (*bundles* **Pinocchio** *into his arms*)   I'd snatch you right out! But you know I'd never push you into the sea. Only a real (*quick decision about a child-friendly word*) butthead would do that!

Pinocchio   A butthead! (**Pinocchio** *has never heard anything so funny.*)

Geppetto   Butthead means –

Pinocchio   I get it! I get it! That's the best word I ever heard.

Geppetto   I think it's OK for you to say butthead. Just to me. Just … you know, like that, as a kind of example.

Oh I don't know. I wish the Blue Fairy had left some rules about what being good means, just so we know where we are.

Pinocchio   Can you teach me all the words?

Geppetto   No, Pinocchio, I don't know all the words.

Pinocchio   Then I don't want to know all the words either.

Geppetto   Ah, but it's so good to learn words! It's so good to learn as much as you can, reading and writing, and arithmetic, and geography, just loads – things you learn when you go to school. You need a proper teacher to learn those things, not just your old father.

Pinocchio   But I just want to stay here with you and look at the sea.

Geppetto   I'd much rather that too, Pinocchio! I just want to watch you understand things. And see things for the first time.

But I think that would be a bit selfish of me, you know. It's really important for you to learn from people who aren't just me.

And besides, I need to work.

Pinocchio   Why do you need to work?

Geppetto   So I can take care of us all! Winter is a hard season, Pinocchio, I need to make sure we have enough of everything before it properly comes. And that means we need money.

(*Becoming palpably more stressed over the course of this speech.*) And you know, Christmas is coming, and I hate the idea of any of the kids in town not having the gifts they really want. So sometimes you need to let the parents pay their money in instalments, or on account – you know, once they can. But that can be a bit harder for us, so, I need to think about that ...

Pinocchio   I have so much to learn from you, Papa! I can just stay with you!

Geppetto   Here's something you can learn. People say I'm too soft a touch. You know, I let other people get their way too easily.

I don't think I can do that anymore.

I think if I'm gonna really teach you to not lie and be a good boy, I need to lay down the law.

I have to! For your sake! Or God knows what will happen!

Even if it's not really my nature.

Pinocchio   What's laying down the law?

Geppetto   Well ...

Quick change to the next scene.

Act Two

Scene One

Geppetto's *cottage*.

Pinocchio   But WHY do I have to go to school?

Geppetto   We've talked about this. All children need to go to school.

Pinocchio   So why doesn't Marmalade have to go to school?

Geppetto   Marmalade's a cat.

Pinocchio   I'm a doll!

Geppetto   You're going to be a real boy before you know it. You have to go to school.

Pinocchio   Yeah but right now I'm not a real boy, why do I have to go to school?

Geppetto   You don't want to be behind, do you?

You don't want the other children to make fun of you?

Pinocchio   Are the other children gonna make fun of me at school?

Geppetto   No! No they definitely won't.

Pinocchio   What if they can tell if I'm made out of wood?

Geppetto   They won't mind. The children in this village are good kids and they don't mind if someone is different.

Pinocchio   Well you can say that.

Geppetto   I know that! I'm a toymaker, the kids in the village are around all the time.

Pinocchio   On their best behaviour maybe. To get nice toys from their parents maybe.

Geppetto   I promise it seems scarier than it is.

I promise.

Pinocchio   What's 'promise'?

Geppetto   When you promise something – it's like you're saying, it's definitely true. Or I'll definitely do it.

Pinocchio   So you promise school isn't scary.

Geppetto   Yes. I promise.

Beat.

Pinocchio   Can't I go tomorrow though?

Geppetto   I think it'll feel scarier if you wait til tomorrow. Plus I can't look after you today, it's nearly Christmas shopping season, I need to get things done.

Look, take Marmalade to school, he'll be there if you get anxious.

Marmalade   Oh yeah, I love going to school! Let's go together, come on, come on –

Marmalade *pushes his face into* **Pinocchio***, directing him until he's out the door.*

Scene Two

On the forest road, to school.

Pinocchio   I thought Geppetto said you didn't need to go to school cause you're a cat. Why do you love school?

Marmalade   School is amazing! There are mice, and in the high corners there are spiders sometimes, and sometimes – there's the most dangerous pudding of all – scorpions!

Pinocchio   Is danger a good thing in a pudding?

Marmalade   Oh yes! Dangerous puddings are the best puddings of all!

Pinocchio   Dunno if I can believe what you say about school now.

Marmalade   Trust me, school is just adventures and cuddles and murder, all my favourite things. I'll go to school with you every day if you want!

Oh no. Danger. Bad danger.

Pinocchio   What?

Marmalade   Polpetta. She always wants to pet me, but her mum's the sweet seller and her hands are always sticky and horrible! I'll follow you but I have to hide!

Polpetta *enters. She wears a dress that looks like a stack of pink doilies and has enormous ribbons in her hair. She is a very loud and correct young lady.*

Marmalade (*as he runs*)   Watch out for her hands!

Polpetta (*loudly, correctly*)   It's the wooden boy Geppetto made!

Pinocchio   Er . . .

Polpetta   Oh I'm so excited, the wooden boy, we can walk to school together and everyone will know I am friends with the wooden boy!

Pinocchio   Are we friends?

Polpetta   Best friends.

Pinocchio   Oh.

Polpetta   Best, most intimate friends. (*She links arms with him. He takes care to avoid her hands.*) What's your name?

Pinocchio   Pinocchio.

Polpetta   I'm Polpetta. Isn't this fun?

Pinocchio (*lying*)   Yes.

His conscience starts to buzz.

Polpetta   You live with that nice ginger cat don't you?
He's so fluffy!

Pinocchio   He is really fluffy!

Polpetta   I think he hates me.

Pinocchio   Er ... he doesn't *hate* you!

The conscience buzzes louder.

Polpetta   What's that sound?

Pinocchio   I can't hear anything.

His nose grows. Louder buzzing.

Polpetta   I don't mean to be rude, but has your nose just
gotten quite a lot bigger?

Pinocchio   No!

The nose grows again. The buzzing gets louder.

Polpetta   I don't mean to be rude but have you pooped
your pants?

Pinocchio   No? Wait – (*he checks*) no, definitely not.

Polpetta   It's just that there's this sound, like there are flies
following you –

Pinocchio *doesn't know what to say.*

Polpetta   It's really okay you know. If we're best, most
bosom, intimate friends, you can always explain what's
going on with you. I promise you can.

Pinocchio   Promise?

Polpetta   Promise.

Pinocchio   Okay. That buzzing is my conscience! I'm still learning how to be a human being so my conscience makes a lot of noise, to remind me to be a good boy so I can become real!

Polpetta (*loudly, correctly*)   FASCINATING.

Polpetta   Here we are.

Pinocchio   This is school?

Marmalade   Yes! Time for murder!

Marmalade *runs off*. **Mommo**, *a horrible bully, enters.*

Mommo   Eww, is that the wooden boy with Polpetta?

Polpetta   Never you mind, Mommo.

Mommo   It is! It is the wooden boy!

Mommo *knocks on* **Pinocchio**'s *head and it makes a loud, satisfying bop.*

Mommo   Ha ha!

Pinocchio   Why are you doing that?

Mommo   It make such a good sound! Listen everyone!

Loud wooden-sounding bop. Everyone – including **Polpetta**, *guiltily – laughs.*

Pinocchio   Get off me! What's wrong with you?

Mommo   I've never seen a wooden boy before! A piece of wood just knocking around!

Mommo *knocks on* **Pinocchio** *again and again it makes a big resonant sound.*

Pinocchio   You watch out, you knock me and I'll knock you out!

The conscience is loud.

Polpetta   Get away from him.

Mommo   You're not even real. It's not bad to be bad to you because you're not real.

Pinocchio   It's not bad to be bad to you because you're a butthead!

The conscience is louder. The school bell starts to ring.

Mommo   What did you call me?

Polpetta   Let's just go in, Pinocchio –

Pinocchio   I called you a butthead!

Mommo   I'm gonna get you. I'm gonna SET YOU ON FIRE!

Mommo *snaps a twig from* **Pinocchio**'s *hair and sets it on fire. The school bell is ringing and it sounds like an alarm bell.* **Mommo** *chases* **Pinocchio**.

Pinocchio   Oh no, school *is* full of murder!

Fratello (*an unseen voice, from the bushes*)   Come over here, kid! Get out of there!

Pinocchio *runs away from school,* **Polpetta** *and* **Mommo** *and towards the unknown voice. He sees a man with a golden glittery beard by the side of the road.*

Fratello   That Mommo is a nasty kid, huh?

Pinocchio   He was really gonna set me on fire!

Fratello   School can be scary, huh?

Pinocchio   Yeah.

I was telling my dad, I thought people might be a bit funny to me, and he said everyone was nice in this town.

He PROMISED. How could he break his promise?

Fratello   Who's your dad?

Pinocchio   Geppetto.

Fratello   Geppetto.

The toymaker.

Of course!

So let me just –

He starts grabbing **Pinocchio** *and examining him closely – by the elbow, by the shirt, shaking him upside down.*

Pinocchio   Erm – I'm sorry sir but could you not –

Fratello   You really are all made of wood!

Pinocchio   Yes!

Fratello   I knew Geppetto was a master. But I never knew he could make anything like this.

How did he make it so you can talk?

Pinocchio   He wished on the Blue Fairy.

Fratello   Yeah I wouldn't expect you'd know.

Pinocchio   I do know! He wished on the Blue Fairy!

Fratello   I should introduce myself – I'm Fratello, the travelling toy seller.

So you've really come to the right place!

I'll teach you loads. Things you'll never learn in school. Real-life things.

Pinocchio   Will real-life things help me become real?

Fratello (*no idea what* **Pinocchio**'s *on about*)   Definitely! Let's hit the road!

Scene Three

On the road.

Pinocchio   I can see so many things I've never seen before!

Fratello   Yes, these are all the houses of the village, and that's the fountain where everyone gets water.

Pinocchio   Who are the people in the fountain?

Fratello   They're not people, they're putti, little angels.

Pinocchio   Don't they get tired, pouring water like that?

Fratello   No. They're made of stone. They look like human beings but they can't move.

Pinocchio   Maybe I'll become like that.

Fratello   What do you mean?

Pinocchio   If I'm bad. I'll become like that. On Christmas.

Fratello   So ... if you're bad, then – on Christmas. You'll become, just a very well-made, life-size, ordinary toy?

Pinocchio   Yes.

Fratello   Interesting!

Pinocchio   Why is that interesting?

Fratello   Do you know why my name is Fratello, Pinocchio?

Pinocchio   No.

Fratello   Because I'm your brother, I'm everyone's brother.

Let me tell you about the toy-selling business, Pinocchio. Some things that your old stick-in-the-mud Geppetto – (*clocks that* **Pinocchio***'s a kind of stick*) sorry, nothing against sticks, obviously – would never tell you.

I see new things and new people every day! So whatever I say to people, it doesn't matter, because I'll never see them again! You can get people to do whatever you want!

You don't need to go to school! You can just – see people, and talk to people, and they'll want to buy toys from you!

Pinocchio   So I'll get the money?

Fratello   Well … technically I'll get the money, but only for now, because I'm showing you the ropes! You wouldn't know a thing about selling toys if it wasn't for me!

Pinocchio   That's true.

Fratello   Imagine if you were stuck in school with that weird nerd Polpetta.

Pinocchio   Ugh. Yeah.

Fratello   All teachers have terrible breath, too. Bet Geppetto didn't tell you that. They all have terrible breath because they drink too much coffee and they're always breathing chalk dust. And then they sneeze. And they get snot and horrible breath all over you.

Pinocchio   I hate bad breath!

Fratello   School is just bad breath on legs!

Song: The Realest Thing of All.

Fratello (*spoken with music under*)   You want to be real, don't you?

Pinocchio   Yes!

Fratello (*singing*)
    I'll tell you what's real
    What's real is what you feel
    The realest thing of all
    Is doing what you want!
    What you want
    Is what I want,
    I can tell
    Is school what you want?

All bullying and taunt,
You want to see the world and sell it tat it doesn't need!
What you want
Is what I want,
I can tell

Pinocchio (*speaking*)   Geppetto says –

Fratello (*speaking*)   'Geppetto says!' Let me ask you does it even count as doing a good thing if you don't really *want* to do it off your own back?

Pinocchio (*speaking*)   ... Oh no.

But – wait –

Pinocchio (*singing*)   I *want* to make Geppetto proud!

Fratello (*singing*)   And why not? You should say it loud!

But would make him prouder than to help a friend in need (*gestures at himself*)?

Pinocchio and Fratello (*singing*)
What you want
Is what I want
I can tell

Fratello (*singing*)   The realest thing of all

Pinocchio (*singing*)   is doing what you want!

Pinocchio and Fratello (*singing*)
What you want
Is what I want
I can tell

The end of the number is marked by an explosion of beautiful curly wood shavings, falling like confetti or snow. When the confetti clears –

INTERVAL!

Scene Four

Geppetto's *cottage. He's sweeping up the wood shavings from a good day's work.* **Marmalade** *enters, twigs caught in his fur. He immediately starts grooming himself.*

Geppetto   My sweet Marmalade! But why are you here without Pinocchio?

Marmalade   Well I got him to school but then I got busy because there were so many mice.

Geppetto   I hope he's not had any trouble.

Pinocchio *enters, flushed with excitement.*

Geppetto   There you are! Oh this is wonderful, you're safe and sound, how was your day?

Pinocchio   It was wonderful!

Geppetto   That's fantastic! What was your favourite part?

Pinocchio   The bad breath.

His conscience buzzes and his nose grows a bit.

Geppetto   What?

Pinocchio   The – (*he grabs another broom to help sweep up but also conceal his face*) the teachers all had bad breath. It really helps me learn.

Mushroom sprouty nose.

Focuses.

The mind!

Geppetto   Uh huh.

What did you learn about?

Pinocchio   The main thing I learned was that if you want to get someone to buy a toy, you have to put it in their child's hand.

That makes it harder for the parents to say no.

They have to not only say no, they have to actually take the toy away from the child, and that hurts their feelings, kind of.

Or it makes the child cry sometimes, to have a lovely toy in their hands – and then, the people they love most take it away.

And parents hate to see their children cry, so they'll spend money they don't even really have to keep the child sweet.

Geppetto Hmm.

What a thing to learn, Pinocchio.

I wasn't expecting you to have learned something like that on your first day of school.

Pinocchio Yeah it's really useful, isn't it.

Geppetto I don't think it is, Pinocchio. You've just told me you learned how to make a child cry today. And how to make people spend money they don't have. I don't think those are useful things to learn.

Pinocchio I also learned that the road to the next village takes me an hour to walk!

Geppetto Does it now?

Pinocchio Yeah we went on a field trip.

Mushroom nose kicking off again.

Geppetto To the next village.

Pinocchio Yes. And we're going on another field trip tomorrow!

A loud and correct knock.

Polpetta *enters.* **Marmalade** *runs up the carved tree, grooming himself, as if he's always been there and isn't just running from* **Polpetta***'s sticky hands.*

Polpetta (*loudly, correctly*)   Hello Geppetto! Hello Pinocchio! Hello – oh, why are you up there Marmalade?

Marmalade   No reason, just … going somewhere you can't get to … licking my own butthole … normal.

Polpetta   I brought you the homework –

Pinocchio   Oh great, let's – let's go outside –

Geppetto   Why did you bring him the homework?

Pinocchio   No reason!

Polpetta   I don't want him to fall behind –

Pinocchio   LET'S GO NOW POLPETTA!

Geppetto   Why would he fall behind?

Polpetta   That horrible Mommo tried to set him on fire and he ran away with Fratello.

Geppetto   Fratello, the toy seller?

You didn't go to school.

You lied.

Pinocchio   … I did lie. I'm sorry.

His nose goes back to normal. He touches it.

Geppetto   Your nose, Pinocchio –

Pinocchio   It goes back to normal if I tell the truth!

Geppetto (*really hurt*)   But wait a minute, Pinocchio – I can't believe you lied straight to my face about your whole day at school! You just made things up!

Polpetta   It wasn't his fault he ran away. Mommo was being really scary.

Geppetto   If people are being scary in school you find a teacher, you don't run away. And you certainly don't lie about it afterward, I'm here to *help* you.

Pinocchio   Then why did *you* lie?

Geppetto   What??

Pinocchio   You promised school wouldn't be scary and it was actually way scarier than I even imagined!

Geppetto   But that's not a lie! How was I supposed to know Mommo would be really scary!

Pinocchio   Well you shouldn't promise then!

Geppetto   Don't talk back to me. Good children don't talk back to their parents and they don't lie. You have to be good or you won't become real! Do you want to just be a heap of sticks again come Christmas?

Pinocchio   No!

Geppetto   No, no, it's too horrible to even think about!

Listen to me, you can't ever see Fratello again, ever, you understand?

Pinocchio   He's – nice – he tells me the truth about things –

Geppetto   He taught you to make children cry! How could that ever be a good thing! Polpetta, I'm really serious about this now. Make sure he doesn't see Fratello again. We have to establish good habits or –

Pinocchio   Or what?

Geppetto   Good friends help you make good choices.

Pinocchio, please. You have me scared.

For your old father. Please promise you'll go to school, and you won't go off with Fratello again.

Pinocchio   I promise.

The soft buzzing of his conscience.

Scene Five

On the road to school. Music under.

Marmalade   Now, Pinocchio really meant it when he
promised he would be good! And did his best to stick to his
promise, he really did. But it wasn't easy.

Musical montage. They're in school and **Mommo** *shoots a spitball
at* **Pinocchio***!*

Pinocchio, **Marmalade**, **Polpetta** (*singing*)   Sometimes you
lie when you're scared.

Pinocchio (*singing*)
    When you spit at me,
    I grow like a tree!
    When I'm bigger than you,
    I'll batter you blue!

Pinocchio, **Marmalade**, **Polpetta** (*singing*)   Sometimes you
lie when you're scared.

Spoken interlude.

Polpetta   School's great though 'cause you get to
understand more about the world. You get to know more
about what's real and what's not.

Pinocchio   Let me ask you something, Polpetta. I'm only
going to become real if I don't tell lies.

What does lying have to do with being real?

Polpetta (*as if she's about to start a verse*)   Well …

Pinocchio *has asked* **Polpetta** *a question she doesn't know the
answer to and she hates it. Again, as if she's about to start a verse …*

Polpetta   The thing is – (*again, as if she's about to start a verse,
but she has nothing.*)

Pinocchio   Yes?

Polpetta   Ooh I can't put it into words. Leave it with me.

Pinocchio, **Marmalade**, **Polpetta** (*singing*)   Sometimes you lie to be nice.

Pinocchio (*singing*)   Yes that looks great.

Polpetta (*singing*)   Your nose is –

Pinocchio (*singing*; *covering his nose, too slowly*)   Too late!

Pinocchio, **Marmalade**, **Polpetta** (*singing*)   Sometimes you lie to be nice.

Pinocchio *and* **Polpetta** *go back to school.* **Fratello** *bribes* **Pinocchio** *and* **Polpetta** *with chocolate to come and sell toys.*

Pinocchio, **Marmalade**, **Polpetta** (*singing*)   Sometimes you lie to make good.

Polpetta (*singing*)
Do your children fight
All day and all night?

Pinocchio (*singing*; *showing one of the toys for sale*)
Buy this to end strife,
It could save your life!

Pinocchio, **Marmalade**, **Polpetta** (*singing*)   Sometimes you lie to make good

Polpetta *and* **Pinocchio** *have their faces covered in chocolate.* **Geppetto** *pops up.*

Polpetta *freezes. She has broken her promise and knows it.*

Geppetto (*speaking*)   So you're saying that's school chocolate?

Pinocchio (*speaking*)   YES.

More music. **Polpetta** *slinks off, ashamed. Buzzing conscience! Mushroom nose! And since there's no* **Polpetta** *to be the voice of reason,* **Fratello** *sneaks* **Pinocchio** *away and out on the open road.*

Fratello (*singing*)
But mostly you lie to get what you want.
There is always a reason to lie.

Pinocchio (*singing*)
    Yes, mostly you lie to get what you want.
    There is always a reason to lie.

Back to speaking.

Pinocchio   Tell me something, Fratello. The Blue Fairy says that if I lie, I won't become real. What does lying have to do with being real?

Fratello   Eh, what's so great about being real anyway?

No, it's better to be an enchanted toy for as long as it lasts and devil take anyone who tells you different!

Pinocchio   Where are we going today, Fratello?

Fratello   Has Geppetto told you about the castle?

Pinocchio   The castle by the sea? Where the Duchess lives?

Fratello   Yes! We're going to see the Duchess! It's a really big thing for me.

Pinocchio   A big thing for us!

Fratello   Yeah! Sure!

Scene Six

Fratello and **Pinocchio** *are in the Castle. Heavy, Romanesque, and dark. The hall is lit by torches and there are streaks of moisture glittering on the walls.*

Pinocchio   Ugh, this place smells like egg on a poop!

Fratello   SHHH. It's just very old.

*At first we hear the **Duchess'** voice without seeing her.*

Duchess   You're late, Fratello.

The **Duchess** *enters, accompanied by a bowing and scraping* **Major-Domo**.

Duchess   I expected you days ago.

Fratello   Sorry Ma'am, it took me more time than expected to – gather the goods.

Duchess   It's nearly Christmas. Apollonia has already missed out on some of her pre-Christmas gifts!

Fratello   You know I'd never want Apollonia to miss out on a pre-Christmas gift!

Duchess   Well then WHY HAVE YOU BEEN SO SLOW? The TORTURES my daughter has been through, Fratello!

Fratello   All of her tortures are over! I've found her the best toy in the world.

Duchess   The best toy in the world? I would give anything to give my daughter the best toy in the world!

Fratello   Pinocchio, come here. Let the Duchess look at you.

Pinocchio *is not sure he likes this*.

Fratello   Come on now, Pinocchio. Don't you need to be a good boy?

Pinocchio *is a bit confused and upset, but steps forward*.

The **Duchess** *comes closer*.

Duchess   The workmanship is exquisite.

Whose is this?

Fratello   Geppetto's, Ma'am.

Duchess   Yes, yes, I can see his hand in this.

Fratello   Geppetto always works with love, Ma'am.

Pinocchio, a good boy would say good evening to the Duchess.

Pinocchio   Good evening.

Fratello   Call her Ma'am.

Pinocchio   Ma'am!

Fratello   No, no, you say 'good evening, Ma'am'.

Pinocchio   Good evening, Ma'am.

Fratello   You see, he's a quick learner.

Duchess   What is the mechanism?

Fratello   I've not been able to work it out, Ma'am. I've never seen anything like it.

Duchess   It seems so responsive!

Fratello   It is, it really is.

Pinocchio   Why are you calling me it?

Duchess   I must have it for Apollonia.

Pinocchio   Are you talking about me?

Fratello   How much?

Duchess   Its weight in gold. Do you have scales?

Fratello *begins to assemble a large, skanky-looking pair of scales from inside his pack, big enough to weigh a human.*

Fratello   I am – honoured by your generous offer, Ma'am. But surely it's worth more than that?

Duchess   I do not haggle, as you know.

Fratello   But surely a diamond or three –

Pinocchio   What are you talking about, I need to go home to my dad.

Fratello   Pinocchio, you have to understand. This kind of money will change my whole life!

Pinocchio   I'm not for sale!

Fratello   It's not as if you're even real. (*This hits* **Pinocchio** *in a way he doesn't expect.*) Have some perspective.

Duchess   Do you know if it'd still be able to talk if you tore its head off?

Fratello   Haven't tried it yet.

Duchess   Apollonia is going through a real tearing-heads-off phase right now.

Fratello   Oh, how sweet!

From offstage, **Apollonia** *screams.*

Duchess   Coming, darling!

Pinocchio   You can't do this!

Fratello   Get on the scales, then, Pinocchio, and be a good boy.

Pinocchio   No!

He pushes the scales at **Fratello** *and runs.* **Fratello** *gets tangled in the chains. The* **Duchess** *tries to grab at him but then –*

Marmalade *runs out of the darkness, screaming, and attacks them both!*

Marmalade (*a sound reminiscent of an unhinged Miss Piggy*) AAAAAYYAAYAYYAYAYAYAYAYAYYAYAAAAAAAA!

Duchess   My GOWN! That beast has RIPPED my GOWN!

Marmalade   The Castle is one of the best places for dangerous pudding! I know it backward and forward!

Duchess   KILL THAT BEAST!

Fratello (*still tangled in the scales, tripping all over himself*)
Yes, Ma'am!

Help! Please! Help me!

Major-Domo   I don't work for you, so –

Marmalade   Come on, Pinocchio, they'll never catch us!

They run all the way home.

Scene Seven

In the cottage. **Pinocchio** *and* **Marmalade** *run in out of breath.*

Geppetto   Pinocchio! Where have you been!

Pinocchio   I've been to the Castle!

Geppetto (*instantly does not believe him*) Uh huh.

Pinocchio   I have, Papa!

Geppetto   How did you get to the Castle?

Pinocchio   Er – I went on my own.

Geppetto   Come into the light, let me see your nose.

Pinocchio   Please Papa! It was very scary!

Can I just sit down or – [have a hot chocolate]

Geppetto   Yes. You can sit down.

Why did they let you into the Castle? If you went on
your own?

Pinocchio   …

Geppetto   Another 'field trip'?

Pinocchio (*quietly*)   That's mean.

Geppetto   What was that?

Pinocchio   I said that's mean.

Geppetto   …

Pinocchio   I'm trying to … do better.

Don't hold those old things over me when I'm trying to do better.

Geppetto   Pinocchio, those 'old things' are from yesterday or the day before!

It's the only way I can know you, how you've behaved in the past.

You're not giving me straight answers in this conversation now –

Pinocchio   Because I'm scared!

Geppetto   Scared of what?!

Pinocchio   Of – the Duchess – of – spiders, we ran through a spider hole, it was horrible, scared of you, when you talk that way.

Geppetto   I'm talking this way because – I'm FRUSTRATED, I'm so tired of going round in circles like this –

Pinocchio   The Duchess wanted to buy me! For her horrible daughter Apollonia who rips the heads off dolls!

Geppetto   I know that didn't happen.

Pinocchio (*really outraged*)   It did! It just did!

Geppetto   How did you get in there? How did she find you? How did you escape?

Pinocchio   She found me in the marketplace – (*the nose, the buzz*) – and then Marmalade saved me!

Geppetto   Our cat saved you?

Pinocchio   Marmalade knows every nook and cranny of that castle, he said so, he hunts for horrible things to eat there all the time!

Geppetto   He *said* so?

Pinocchio   Yes!

Geppetto   I'm going to bed, I can't take much more of this.

Pinocchio   No! No! Don't go to bed! I'll set your bed on fire!!

Geppetto   WHAT did you just say?

Pinocchio   I didn't mean it just – don't go to bed! I need comforting! Don't you even want to be a good dad?

Geppetto (*taken aback, outraged*)   Of – course – I want to be a good dad, how can you ask me that – you can't act like this, you'll never become real!

Pinocchio   You're just like Fratello!

Fratello said I'd never become real. I'm not even real so what does it matter if Apollonia tears my head off.

Geppetto   Did you go off with Fratello again is that what you're lying about?

Pinocchio   NO.

The buzz, the nose.

Geppetto   If I never have to hear that noise again in my life –

Pinocchio   FINE!

Pinocchio *squashes his* **Conscience**.

A beat. Then, bedlam. **Geppetto** *is in despair*.

Marmalade (*running in big loops*)   Oh no, oh no, oh no –

Geppetto   Please no, PLEASE no –

Pinocchio   I shouldn't have done that – I shouldn't have done that –

Marmalade   How did you do that! How can anyone be naughty enough to destroy their own conscience! You won't ever become real!

Pinocchio   No, no – I won't ever become real –

Geppetto   That can't be it – that – can't be IT –

Marmalade (*very quietly, putting his face into* **Pinocchio**) We need you here.

How can we go back to life without you?

No, no.

Quiet.

Geppetto   We have to find some way.

Pinocchio   What way?

Geppetto   I don't know! But there's no way this is the end! I'm going to find some way of fixing this, Pinocchio!

Pinocchio   I'm sorry! I'm so sorry!

Geppetto   No time for that now.

Be calm.

Pinocchio   I will be calm, I will be, I promise.

Geppetto   Good. Okay. Good.

Geppetto *takes up a lantern.*

I'm going to go looking for – I don't know. A doctor, a priest, I don't know, some kind of solution. I'll be back in just a minute. But while I'm gone, you can't leave the cottage for any reason. Unless it's on fire.

Pinocchio   How long will you be?

Geppetto   Not long. STAY PUT. When I come back I'll have a plan.

Act Three

Scene One

In the cottage.

Pinocchio   Why isn't he back?

It's been hours now. Why isn't he back?

Marmalade   You should pace around, it'll make you feel better.

Pinocchio   I don't deserve to feel better! I squooshed my conscience.

Marmalade   If you squished your conscience, and you're naughty all through now, why do you feel so bad about it?

Pinocchio   I don't know! I don't know what to do, we promised him not to leave but something really bad must have happened.

Marmalade   I have an idea!

Pinocchio   … What is it?

Marmalade   Let's not make it worse.

Pinocchio   …

Marmalade   No but –

It's nighttime, it's winter, he told us not to leave.

If we go wandering around in the freezing cold we'll be making it worse.

So what can we do that won't make it worse?

Pinocchio   The Blue Fairy! I can still make my one wish on the Blue Fairy!

She can help find Geppetto.

Blue Fairy!

Blue Fairy!

BLUE –

Marmalade   How did we get her to come here last time?

Pinocchio   I don't know, I was still just a heap of sticks.

Marmalade   Geppetto –

Geppetto wished with his whole heart. On the moon. That he would have a child.

Pinocchio   Okay.

Blue Fairy!

Blue Moon!

I wish –

I wish with my whole heart to help Geppetto.

Wherever he is, I want to help him.

I wish to bring him back home safe and sound.

A beat.

With a beautiful whirl, the **Blue Fairy** *appears.*

Pinocchio   You came!

Blue Fairy   Well, you wished with your whole hearts. A whole-hearted wish is a powerful thing.

Pinocchio   Where is Geppetto?

Blue Fairy   In trouble.

Marmalade   Oh no!

Blue Fairy   He went to the Castle, where the mountains meet the sea, he was going to offer to make the Duchess anything she wanted if she would only help you become real. But the Castle is so high up, and it was slippery and dark, and he fell in the sea.

Pinocchio   And it's so cold!

Blue Fairy   Yes, he was stunned, and he got swallowed by a dogfish!

Marmalade   A dogfish?!?

Blue Fairy   He's still alive in the dogfish's belly!

I can take you almost all the way there!

But I can't get my wings wet, if I get my wings wet I can't fly and I'll never be able to go home to the moon.

Pinocchio   How far can you take us?

Blue Fairy   I can take you to the point in the sea where the dogfish is now. But once you touch the sea's surface you're on your own.

Pinocchio   We're going. Right, Marmalade?

Marmalade   I hate water.

And dogs.

A dogfish sounds like the worst kind of thing there is.

They both look at him.

Marmalade   Okay we're going!

Pinocchio   NOW. No time to lose!

*The **Blue Fairy** lifts **Marmalade** and **Pinocchio** in her magnificent claws/mandibles and they are flying over land and sea.*

Scene Two

Flying over land and sea.

Pinocchio   The village looks so small from here!

Look at the Christmas lights.

The sea is so dark and cold.

Blue Fairy   The sea looks dark because you can see the lights of the village.

It's a blue moon night.

Let your eyes adjust to the moonlight when you're out to sea and you'll be able to see the dogfish when you get there.

And he'll be quite eager to eat you up!

With a splash, **Pinocchio** *and* **Marmalade** *hit the choppy water. It's loud and rough.*

Marmalade   I HATE THIS! I HATE THIS! I ABSOLUTELY HATE THIS!

Pinocchio   Be brave!

It's time!

They plunge into the moonlit waters – down, down, down.

It is terribly silent, apart from the roar of blood in their heads and the pressure ringing in their ears.

A great dark shape emerges behind them.

It is the **Dogfish** *– which, contrary to its name, is actually a kind of large shark.*

Marmalade   That's not a dogfish, that's a shark!

Pinocchio   A dogfish is a kind of shark!

Marmalade   NO! No way, this is too much, it's a fish and a dog and a shark, no!

Pinocchio   Come on, Marmalade! This is your moment – be a dangerous pudding.

A stirring strain of music.

Marmalade   Yes.

Dear God, yes.

I am the child of lions, my whole life has lead me here –

Today, *I* am the dangerous pudding.

(*To the* **Dogfish**.) Come at me you villain! AAAAAH!

The **Dogfish** *swallows them whole.*

Scene Three

In the darkness of the **Dogfish**'s *belly.*

Vast ribs, glowing fish skeletons underfoot.

Marmalade   Being inside a fish is the worst thing that's ever happened to me.

Geppetto   Hello?!

Pinocchio   Papa!

Geppetto   Pinocchio. What are you doing here?

Pinocchio   We came to save you –

Geppetto   I told you to stay in the house! You promised! You lied! I knew you would lie and you lied! Why do you never ever do what I say! This is so dangerous, Pinocchio!

Pinocchio   The Blue Fairy said it was all right!

The Blue Fairy took us here!

Geppetto   Will you stop lying, Pinocchio?

Everyone knows fairies can't fly when their wings are wet!

Pinocchio   She dropped us on the surface.

Marmalade   Ugh! Licking salt water out of fur. Ugh ugh ugh.

Gags and spits as only a cat can.

Geppetto   Well – I don't know how else you could have found me – I just don't know what to believe.

Pinocchio   Sometimes it feels like I can tell the truth and it doesn't even matter.

I wished to find you with my whole heart.

Geppetto   Oh Pinocchio.

But you know – you only get one wish on the Blue Fairy, Pinocchio. Why didn't you wish to become real?

Pinocchio   I – don't know. It didn't – [seem important? No, that's not it.]

I knew you'd never be gone for so long unless there was something really wrong. I just wanted you to be okay.

Geppetto   Come here, Pinocchio.

Let me see your face.

Geppetto *lifts his lantern to* **Pinocchio**'s *face. His nose is normal, he is telling the truth, he looks almost real.*

Geppetto   You are a very brave boy, Pinocchio. I'm sorry I didn't believe you before. I'm lucky to have a child like you.

Pinocchio   I should have wished for her to get us out as well. Now we're stuck.

Geppetto   Hmm. I just don't think the Blue Fairy would have taken you somewhere you couldn't get out of, you know? So there must be a way out.

Pinocchio   What if the dogfish has loose teeth? We can just charge our way out!

Geppetto   That's what I was thinking! But I've checked every tooth, they're all rock-hard and shut tight, it's no good.

Pinocchio *looks very down.*

Geppetto   No, no, but that was a very good idea! Let's keep thinking, together we'll find a way. What else do you think might help?

Pinocchio   Well, what tools do we have?

Geppetto   Such a good question! I've been thinking, if only I had some of my carpentry tools – but I only brought a lantern.

Marmalade   I brought my claws! I'm extremely savage!

Pinocchio   We know you're very savage, Marmalade – (**Geppetto** *clocks this exchange and begins to think* **Pinocchio** *may not quite be lying about understanding* **Marmalade**) – but you know what else you can make people do – sneeze!

Marmalade   That is an amazing power, you're right, I'm amazing.

Marmalade *tries to make the* **Dogfish** *sneeze.*

Geppetto   I see! If the dogfish sneezed hard enough, he'd definitely spit us out! He wouldn't be able to help it!

But how do we make him sneeze with just a lantern?

Pinocchio   We don't just have a lantern.

We also have a bit of damp wood.

Pinocchio *snaps off a handful of his hair and drops it in the lantern.*

Geppetto   Oh no, what are you doing?

Pinocchio   Just seeing if it'll make smoke.

He blows on the twigs and makes a little glow.

Blow on it, help it catch.

Geppetto   I don't like this at all –

Pinocchio   It's okay, Papa. I *promise*.

Promise-promise.

Geppetto *takes a beat. He knows he must trust* **Pinocchio**.

He and **Pinocchio** *blow on the twigs. Smoke begins to twirl up from their hands.*

The vast ribs of the **Dogfish** *buckle.*

Marmalade   Dogfish doesn't like that!

They blow at the blaze to keep it going.

Geppetto   Oh come on, come on –

The **Dogfish** *sneezes.*

It's a horrible cataclysm. Everyone stumbles.

Pinocchio   Remember, when you hit the water, swim towards the moon!

The **Dogfish** *sneezes them right out of his belly, and into the cold waters of the Adriatic.*

Scene Four

The cottage. **Pinocchio** *and* **Geppetto** *are wrapped in blankets and drinking from steaming mugs.* **Marmalade** *is curled up and lapping at a small dish of milk. The* **Blue Fairy** *is also there.*

Pinocchio   Thank you for flying us back, Blue Fairy.

This is very good hot chocolate.

Marmalade   And thanks for getting me lactose-free milk, I do appreciate it.

Blue Fairy   I'm just so glad you're back safe and sound.

Geppetto   That was a very brave thing you did, Pinocchio.

You sacrificed yourself – so we could get home safe.

Pinocchio   ...

Geppetto   What's wrong?

Pinocchio   I don't know.

The twigs – my hair – when you burn them, they just disappear.

Geppetto   Yes.

Pinocchio   To exist – and then – to not exist, it's too much! I don't know! What does it mean to be real?

Pause.

Geppetto   All of your actions are real.

The effect they have on other people is real.

If you lie – if you act like your behaviour doesn't affect other people –

Pinocchio   It's like wishing you weren't real, and they weren't real, like they were just toys to be played with. And put away.

When I hurt you – is it because I'm real?

Geppetto   Yes.

Pinocchio   Then I don't want to be real. And I don't want you to be real either.

Marmalade *almost intervenes. The* **Blue Fairy** *stops him.*

Geppetto   I would rather be hurt by you than you just be a toy.

A thousand times. A thousand times.

Any hurt I ever get from you is so tiny compared to how much I love you.

But I want you to always tell the truth. When you lie to me, it's like you're pretending to be someone you're not.

And I love the real you.

Blue Fairy   Geppetto's wish, the only wish of his life, has come true.

Spirals and sparks come off **Pinocchio**. *He is briefly invisible in a flash of light. When the blaze dims, light shines on him differently. He's not made of wood – he is now a soft animal. The* **Blue Fairy** *has disappeared.*

Pinocchio   Papa! I'm soft like you! Am I real?

Geppetto   Yes, I think you are real!

Marmalade (*circling them, bumping his sides against everyone*)
I'm real! I'm also real!

Geppetto (*scratching his head*)   You're a good boy,
Marmalade.

To go into the freezing sea after me like that!

Marmalade   I'm very excited! I want to gnaw you! Because
I love you!

Geppetto (*pulls him off by the scruff of his neck*)   No biting
now, no biting! I nearly lost you both!

Marmalade (*going limp*)   Ohh, I'm very calm suddenly and
I don't know why.

Polpetta *bursts in*.

Polpetta   Pinocchio! I've figured it out! I know what lying
has to do with being real!

Geppetto   But we just –

Pinocchio   I want to hear this!

Polpetta   It's really lonely if you just lie all the time. And
cheat people because you can. You don't live in the world
with everyone else.

The more other people are real to you, the more real you
become.

Pinocchio   Polpetta – I'm lucky to have a friend like you.

Polpetta   Can I pet Marmalade?

Marmalade   FINE.

Marmalade *is fussed over, the centre of attention, just as it
should be.*

Marmalade   So that was the story of how one Christmas, Pinocchio became a real human being, and Geppetto became a father, and Marmalade was still the best!

Musical reprise/curtain call.

Pinocchio (*singing*)   Sometimes you lie when you're scared!

Geppetto (*singing*)   Sometimes you lie as a wish!

Pinocchio (*singing*)   Sometimes you wish you're not real.

Marmalade (*singing*)   Inside the guts of a fish!

Everyone (*singing*)
    But often you lie
    Because you're afraid
    Because you're afraid and alone.
    When others are real, then so are you
    To be loved, you must be known.

    When others are real, then so are you
    To be loved, you must be known.

Christmas lights go on. It's the curtain-call-song!

Pinocchio   I LOVE BEING REAL! What else is real?

Everyone (*singing*)
    Bullies are real, but so's hot chocolate
    Dogfish are real, but so is laughter
    Hurt and loneliness are so real
    But so is Happily Ever After.

    So is Happily Ever After,
    Make sure what you say is true,
    And if anyone gives you trouble,
    Say Pinocchio told you to!